Let's Go!

The Story of Getting from There to Here

Lizann Flatt

Illustrated by
Scot Ritchie

MAPLE
TREE
PRESS

Maple Tree Press Inc.
51 Front Street East, Suite 200, Toronto, Ontario M5E 1B3
www.mapletreepress.com

Distributed in Canada by Raincoast Books
9050 Shaughnessy Street, Vancouver, British Columbia V6P 6E5

Distributed in the United States by Publishers Group West
1700 Fourth Street, Berkeley, California 94710

Dedication
To Mom and Dad, for helping me get from there to here.

Acknowledgments
The author gratefully acknowledges the financial support of the Ontario Arts Council,
and wishes to thank her editor, Anne Shone, for her insight and endless patience.

Cataloguing in Publication Data
Flatt, Lizann
Let's go : the story of getting from there to here / Lizann Flatt ; illustrator, Scot Ritchie.

ISBN 13: 978-1-897349-02-1 / ISBN 10: 1-897349-02-5

1. Transportation-History-Juvenile literature.   I. Ritchie, Scot   II. Title.
TA1149.F53 2007   j388.09   C2007-901792-4

Design & art direction: Claudia Dávila
Illustrations: Scot Ritchie

We acknowledge the financial support of the Canada Council for the Arts, the Ontario
Arts Council, the Government of Canada through the Book Publishing Industry
Development Program (BPIDP), and the Government of Ontario through the Ontario
Media Development Corporation's Book Initiative for our publishing activities.

ONTARIO ARTS COUNCIL
CONSEIL DES ARTS DE L'ONTARIO

Printed in China

A   B   C   D   E   F

When you want to go to school or play at a friend's house, you can get there by catching a bus, climbing into a car, or hopping on a bicycle.

But what if there were no cars or buses or bikes? What if you could walk, but there were no streets, no sidewalks, no signs?

There once was a time like that here in North America. Come follow the story of how traveling changed, and how that changed everything.

Once when this world was cold,
walking was the way people traveled.

With
soft
footfalls

they followed food, hunted herds,
wandering through the wilderness.

The land slowly warmed. The people walked with packs on their backs.

Some trailed travois,

pulled toboggans,
wore snowshoes.

In quiet canoes made from forest trees,
they crossed lakes, rode rivers,
and skimmed the shores.

Then one day,
blown on strong ocean winds.

from the lands of the kings and the queens,

sailing ships slid swiftly to shore.
The men who explored found riches
in fishes, riches in furs, and riches
in timber from trees.

Fur traders, trappers, and mappers followed
the ways the first peoples traveled in this land.

In canoes full of cargo they crossed

cold clear fresh waters.

They walked ancient paths
through the wild woody green.

A whinny!
A neigh!

What wonderful beasts! Horses stepped out of sailing ships.
At first just a few but the herds slowly grew.

They went faster and farther, they helped
with the hunt. Horses to ride, horses to
trade, and horses to tow the travois.

The settlers sailed over.
They'd spent weeks in wood ships,
tossed on the wide open sea.

They **paddled**, they **poled**,
they **sailed** and **they rowed**,
to settle along river banks
and make homes on the shores.

Horses

hauled the settlers'
barges; pulled their goods
at portages.

They helped make the trails.
They towed away trees.

Horses pulled carts, pulled carriages,
coaches, and wagons that
waded for weeks
through flat grassy seas.

Then a sound split the air,
a steam engine stuttered!
Machines with
boiling bellies

bⁱllowed

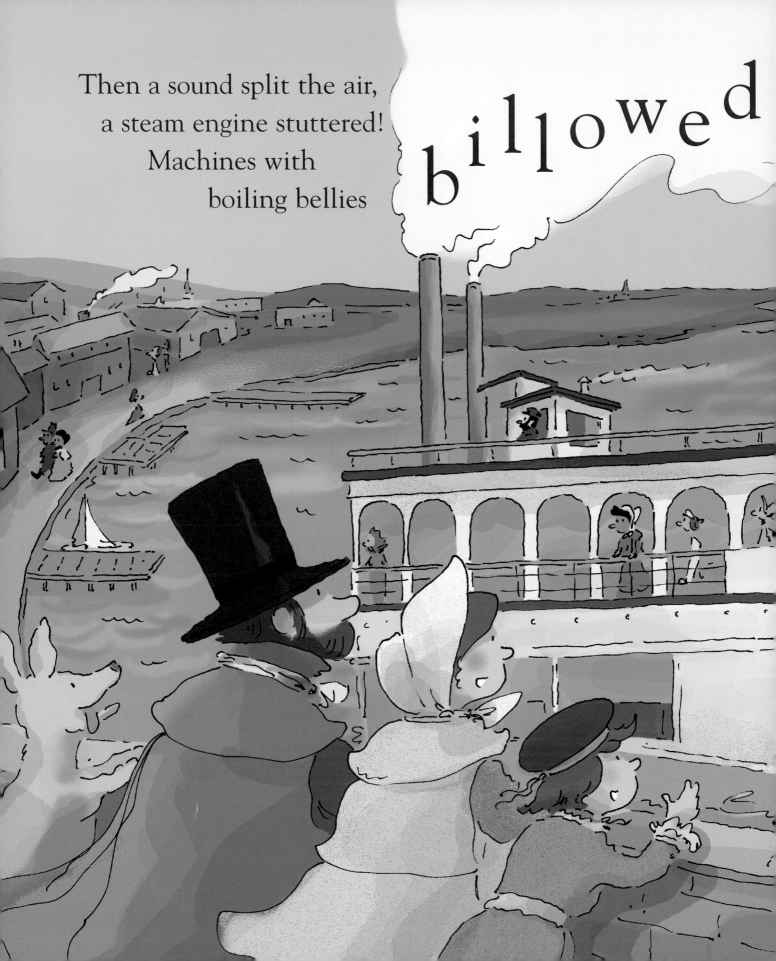

steam!

Paddlewheel steamers
churned up inland waters.
Iron steam ships chewed
the miles of sea.

Forest was felled,
rock blasted away,
then cold metal bands
lined the land.

The trains traveled the tracks,
smoke spewing from stacks.

Like huge iron horses they hauled their long loads,

crossing the country in days!

People settled in cities where steam engines stopped and **the cities swelled up** in size.

STATION

The streets filled with people, with horses, with streetcars. A speedy two-wheeler pedaled in!

Get out of the way!
It's an automobile!

It went faster and farther than a horse or a bike could, on an engine that burned gasoline.

No need for feed and water each day; no fire to stoke to make steam. First just a few for the rich well-to-do, but how noisy and crowded the streets quickly grew.

A noise up above! Machines in the air.

Propeller planes skipped through the skies.

Landing on lonely lakes like gigantic geese,
bushplanes buzzed in with supplies and the mail.

Cars became something that everyone needed.
Cars needed highways, straight streets, big bridges,

and
ribbons of roadways
to tie town to town.

With a deep throaty grumble

the diesel trains ((rumbled))

and steam train's hiss faded away...

Freight trains hauled long lines of cargo by rail, while trucks, tractor-trailers, and tankers took loads, driving on smooth superhighways and roads.

WOW food

Jets chalked the sky with their shattering roars,

winging people

through air at top speeds.

Airports, arrivals, all over the world!
Taking air you'd be there in
just hours, not days.

Ignition! A blast off!.

Riding rockets to space,
astronauts flew past the Moon.
Space travel is new, for only a few.

Will we circle the stars like we now drive our cars? Someday that might become true.

How will you travel when you go out today?
How will *you* get around?
By car, by canoe?
Bike, toboggan, snowshoe?

Get ready,

get set,

now

let's go!

Did You Know?

Many scientists think that the first people came to North America during the Ice Ages by walking from Asia across a bridge of land that is now underwater.

The European explorers were really looking for a fast way to sail to Asia to buy things such as spices, silk, and jewels when they "accidentally" found North and South America.

Horses originally lived in North America but they became extinct here at the end of the last Ice Age. The Spanish explorers brought the first horses back to North America on sailing ships from Europe.

The first peoples made their canoes, snowshoes, toboggans, and travois by hand using materials from trees and animals.

Dogs are related to wolves. They were the first animals to live closely with people. They often pulled travois or toboggans before the arrival of horses. The dog in this book is a Carolina dog, or American dingo, a dog that some scientists think may have come to North America with the first peoples.

A portage is a place where a boat had to be pulled to shore and all the cargo, plus the boat itself, carried on land. This was done to pass by a spot where the water was too shallow or too fast to paddle on, or to get a traveler from one body of water to another.

The word "horsepower" was first used to compare the power of steam engines with the power of horses. A steam engine was stronger than a horse so it had more "horsepower."

Inside a steam locomotive, a fireman kept a wood or coal fire burning to heat water to make the steam that would turn the wheels. Both steam and smoke spewed out of the smokestack.

Steam trains made travel faster, cheaper, and easier than ever before. For the first time many people, not just very rich people, could travel just for fun.

Early roads were mostly single lanes covered with dirt, stones, or logs. They were often so muddy and bumpy, it was much easier to travel by water. That's why the earliest towns and cities were built along river banks, lakeshores, or the sea coasts.

The first steam ships used huge paddlewheels, but in rough waves paddlewheels could be rocked out of the water. Ship builders switched to propellers, which spin underwater at the back of a ship, and worked well even in rough water.

An engineer worked a steam locomotive's controls. A special car called the tender carried a load of coal or wood and water to keep the train going. The caboose, where the train crew ate and slept, was the last car on the train.

The popular "safety bicycle" was safer than the earlier high wheel bicycles. The safety bicycle's chain and gear system meant both wheels could be the same size. Its air-filled tires made for a smoother ride than earlier iron or wood wheels.

Early automobiles, or cars, were engines put on horse carriage or buggy frames. They were nicknamed "horseless carriages" and said to be cleaner than horses because they didn't leave poop on city streets.

Propellers pull planes through the air. Jet engines push planes through the air.

Early planes were not heated and carried only a few people at a time. Often passengers had to sit with the cargo. Modern jets can carry hundreds of people in heated comfort, serving passengers meals and showing movies to help pass the time.

Horses pulled the first streetcars. Electric streetcars, or trolleys, got their electric power from the overhead wires. They made travel within large crowded cities fast and easy.

Small bush planes flew mostly north-south routes because the early railroad lines went mostly east-west. Bush planes had floats to land on lakes in summer and skis to land on them in winter. Bush planes were also used to spot forest fires from the air.

Because space shuttles return to Earth by landing on an airplane runway, they can be flown to space again. Earlier space capsules could only be used once because they returned to Earth by "splashdown," landing in the ocean. They would be too damaged to be used again.